T0208432

DELIVERANCE
the Lost Ministry of Jesus ● ● ● ● ● ● ● ●

John McCartin

WESTBOW
PRESS®
A DIVISION OF THOMAS NELSON
& ZONDERVAN

Contents

Dedication

I would like to dedicate this book to God the Father, Son and Holy Spirit for walking me through a deep deliverance and getting me free.

Preface

[1] I love you, O Lord, my strength.
[2] The Lord is my rock and my fortress and my deliverer,
my God, my rock, in whom I take refuge,
my shield, and the horn of my salvation, my stronghold.
[3] I call upon the Lord, who is worthy to be praised,
and I am saved from my enemies.[1] Ps 18:1–3, ESV

This book came about after a 17-year struggle with Mental Health symptoms. The struggle included a year of a number of symptoms at the end. After going to several programs and ending up on Long Term Disability, the Lord led me into a self-deliverance by casting out demons of mental illness and things got dramatically better. Still having some symptoms, He then walked me through a very thorough deliverance. And now, I'm free. The new way was better than what I had used before. Then the Lord led me to write these steps down in a book.

I hope you are blessed by the discussion and prayer found in this book. It's my prayer that you would find freedom in Christ.

---

[1] *The Holy Bible: English Standard Version*. (2016). (Ps 18:1–3). Wheaton, IL: Crossway Bibles.

Introduction

*15 He said to them, "Go into all the world and preach the gospel to all creation. 16 Whoever believes and is baptized will be saved, but whoever does not believe will be condemned. 17 And these signs will accompany those who believe: **In my name they will drive out demons;** they will speak in new tongues; 18 they will pick up snakes with their hands; and when they drink deadly poison, it will not hurt them at all; they will place their hands on sick people, and they will get well." 2 (Emphasis added.)*

When Jesus started His ministry, he found an Israel that had demon problems. The world is no different today. As we follow in the footsteps of Jesus in our ministry, we find a world full of demon problems also. Disease and even mental illness plague the world. Anger, lust problems and failed marriages are everywhere. We normally don't recognize these as demons, but nothing has changed since Jesus was here. Here in the gospel of Mark, Jesus clearly says that deliverance – driving out demons – is a sign accompanying believers.

When we sin, we give away our authority over ourselves and allow the enemy to gain some control over us through demons. Some sin is more serious than others. Anything that involves the occult or even Satanism gives over significant control to the enemy.

Jesus paid the price for our sin and the blood of Jesus frees us from the guilt of our sin. When we bring the blood of Jesus on us for our sin in confession, we receive forgiveness and freedom from bondage. Deliverance involves

---

2 *The New International Version*. (2011). (Mk 16:15–18). Grand Rapids, MI: Zondervan.

bringing the blood of Jesus on us for our sin, gaining forgiveness from God and gaining freedom from the power of Satan.

Another part of deliverance is getting free from curses. Sometimes when we sin, the sin is so serious that God assigns a curse to us. When we are under a curse, that means that blessing is stopped in some way. The curse could be a medical condition. It could also entail some situation in our lives such as a marital or parental relationship problem. Property like houses, furniture and belongings can come under a curse when the sin occurs using that property or if the property is proximity to the sin.

Since Jesus became a curse on the cross, we can gain freedom of the curse through the blood of Jesus. Once deliverance is farther along it will be important to break curses on yourself and your family if you have a spouse or are a parent. Also, you will need break curses on property and dwellings like houses. One way to break curses is to go through your dwelling to each room. Work through the deliverance prayer to gain forgiveness and freedom from that sin. Then, break the specific curse off the room. Then bless the items in that room and bless the room. After, you've gone through the entire dwelling, break the curse on the dwelling and bless the dwelling. (Note: a prayer will be provided for both breaking a curse and blessing.) Then break the curse on the people. Then bless the people. Then offer a simple prayer dedicating the people and the dwelling to the Lord.

Every time we bring the blood of Jesus on a sin or sin area, it's important to exercise the authority of Jesus given to us as priests of God to break each curse under the authority of Jesus by way of His shed blood on the cross. Sometimes, when breaking a curse, a demon will be expelled from your body during the prayer. When that happens, it's important to complete the entire prayer to complete breaking the curse. This book will outline each type of prayer and each part including breaking a curse.

Also, in every confession of sin or sin area, it is important to cast all demons associated with a sin. Sometimes, a sin does not bring a demon. But it is important to work through the prayer to cast out all demons. There are lower-level demons that report to the higher-level demons. For example, for Halloween a sin with a demon might be carving a pumpkin. So, once all the Halloween sin has been confessed and demons are cast out, the main

Halloween demon can be cast out. Halloween is involved in the occult. To cast the occult demon out, you will need to cleanse all the other occult areas including the specific demons for specific sins or groups of sin. Finally, you can then cast out the demon of the occult. Since all sin is of Satan, you will need to cast out Satanism once everything is cleansed.

Since the enemy wants to keep us in bondage, there is usually a power struggle that occurs when trying to gain deliverance. The enemy will stop at nothing to keep you under bondage. This involves using people who are in bondage to stop you. That can be a friend or family member.

The important thing to remember is that God is sovereign and will make a way for you to repent and confess and get free. While it's not easy, God is there in it all to help you through the Holy Spirit. It's also important to remember that it is the Spirit that performs the deliverance. While you may not have the power to be delivered, the Holy Spirit does. For example, the enemy will try to hide memories of sin from you. The Holy Spirit knows what you need to confess and will remind you of all things.

If you are a husband, it's important to understand that God honors your deliverance for your whole immediate family. While your wife will still need to confess, the power of Satan over your wife is diminished when you pursue deliverance. This is very important for her to get free.

Another important part of deliverance is cleansing of personal belongings. If you own anything tied to sin, that forms a contract with Satan and must be broken. The way to do that is to dispose of the property and bring the blood on the ownership and sin. Sometimes, you may have to go to difficult measures to dispose of the property. Family members under the power of Satan will try to stop you. You must persist. Since God owns everything, He will make a way for you to dispose of the cursed items.

What is not commonly understood is that you can become involved in areas of sin like the occult through holiday participation like Halloween, specific participation in holidays like Santa Clause, movies, books and even games. While it may seem that you are not actually participating, you are and it forms a covenant with Satan that must be broken just as the involvement forms a contract of control. This will also not be easy. But God is faithful and will be there fighting for you the whole time.

Work through each section of the book one at a time. Read about each sin area and try to understand and remember how you've sinned in each area. Keep in mind that as you pray each prayer, you will become freer and you will begin to remember your sin. It may be necessary to repeat certain sections of the prayers before moving on to others.

One other thing to remember is that there is spiritual warfare in deliverance. It's important to stay in prayer and fasting for your deliverance and ask other Christians to pray for you as well. Your church website may have a prayer ministry where you can ask for prayer. If you have a Bible Study, you can ask for prayer from the members. You may want to ask close friends either through email, text or phone call to prayer for specific prayer requests.

Of note is that some sin areas have lists. For your convenience, check boxes have been provided to mark list so you know what to pray for when listing sins.

Now let's pray an opening prayer:

Thank you that Jesus is my Lord and Savior who paid the perfect price for all of my sin. Lord, thank you that the cleansing blood of Jesus covers my sin and that when I confess my sins you will forgive me of my sin and cleanse me of all unrighteousness. Thank you that based on the blood of Jesus, I have the authority to cast out lies, break covenants, break curses and cast out demons. I pray that you would make a way for me and bless me in this deliverance. I pray that you would fight spiritual warfare on behalf of me and my family. Send your angels, Lord.

The Prayers

The following prayer should be prayed for each sin or group of sins. This book will outline each sin area. Each section will include a prayer for a particular sin area. You should go through the prayer for sins as the Holy Spirit reminds you. As you progress through the prayer, the Holy Spirit may remind you of things and you will need to go back to previous sections of the prayer. We will discuss that further after the prayer.

When you bring the blood of Jesus on your sin, it is important that you identify any times when you provided a leadership role. That could include being a bad example to a younger sibling, child, or wife. When you provide a leadership role for sin, you become a "priest of Satan." You are leading others in sin. That must be cleansed and a covenant with Satan must be broken. The prayer will show you how to cleanse and break that.

Here's the main deliverance prayer:

In the name of Jesus, by the blood of Jesus, I bring the cleansing blood of Jesus on me and my family for my involvement in sin of [name sin] including [specific examples], and being a priest of Satan by word or example [in this way]

In the name of Jesus and by the blood of Jesus, I renounce believing the lie that [insert lies]. In the name of Jesus, I command that lie to go to the Abyss and never return. I declare the truth that [insert truth]. (Repeat for more than one lie.)

In the name of Jesus, by the blood of Jesus, I break the covenant I made with Satan [when I was a priest of Satan in that way] and my general involvement in that sin.

In the name of Jesus, by the blood of Jesus, I break the generational curse of [sin area like Halloween or sin or group of sins] off me and my family.

In the name of Jesus, by the blood of Jesus, I break the curse of [sin area like Halloween or sin or group of sins] off me and my family.

In the name of Jesus, by the blood of Jesus, I command a spirit of [sin area or demon the Holy Spirit identifies] to directly to the Abyss and never return. In the name of Jesus, I ask that the Holy Spirit would fill all extra space that there now is.

When breaking a covenant, the Holy Spirit may remind you of sin that you did not confess, commonly being a "priest of Satan" in some way. When that happens go back to bringing the blood on the sin. Pick up by saying "I also bring the blood on sin or sin group including being a priest of Satan [name way.]

When breaking a curse, the Holy Spirit may let you know that the covenant wasn't broken or there was some sin or sin group that still needs cleansing. In either case, go back to the first part of the prayer and bring the blood on the sin or sin area. Then if the covenant needs to be broken, break it and then continue. Or, if just the curse needs to be broken, break the curse. It's possible that you may have to go back to the beginning until everything is broken. Keep cleansing the sin until you can move forward. Then break the covenant or curse.

When praying the prayer to cast out the demon after the curse is broken, a demon will be expelled by the Holy Spirit. As soon as the demon is expelled, stop praying the prayer. You are done with that sin or sin group. You may need to pray the casting out of demons part of the prayer in its entirety before the demon is cast out. If the demon doesn't come out, there may not be a demon. If there is a demon, you may cough or feel a sensation in your chest. If you do, the demon has not come out. You may also need to pray for the casting out. Then, pray a prayer for God to remove the demon. After that, repeat this part of the prayer. A demon will come out.

Sometimes you aren't able to go through the steps. In such time, a general apology such as "Lord, I'm very sorry I did [this.]" can be a way of starting and completing the confession.

Now, depending on what sin area you are working on, you will need to keep going until you confess everything for that sin area. As you complete each heading in each sin area, break the curse for that heading and cast out the demon. Do this for each heading in the Sin area. The following prayer will show you how to do that.

In the name of Jesus, by the blood of Jesus, I break the generational curse of [heading or sin area] off me and my family.

In the name of Jesus, by the blood of Jesus, I break the curse of [heading or sin area] off me and my family.

In the name of Jesus, by the blood of Jesus, I command a spirit of [heading or sin area] to go directly to the Abyss and never return.

Once the demon is out, pray for the Holy Spirit to fill the empty space. You may feel the Spirit as He enters your body.

Lies

Lies started in the garden. Satan lied to Eve and she sinned. The same thing is happening today. We can receive lots of lies from the enemy. We mistakenly assume that it's our thoughts, but in actuality it's from the Enemy -- Satan. Everything that runs across your thinking is not always your thoughts; the thought could come from a demon.

The Bible tells us to take every thought captive. So, when a thought comes across our mind, we should ask the question "is really true" or "is that Godly?"

Lies can come from demons. If you believe and act on a lie long enough the lie demon can be planted within us. Each prayer in this book asks you to identify what is the lie that you believed and may be causing you to sin.

Mental Health

The world has fallen for the lies of psychology and psychiatry. Many people think that psychologists and psychiatrist are just doctors of the mind. However, the teaching of these professionals is not based on the cornerstone of Christ Jesus. They are false teachers. They advocate traditions that are not of God. They are blind guides. They are priests of Satan.

Psychology

Psychology offers a false gospel. Again, Psychologists are false teachers. Psychology promises that you can find happiness if you are able to "cope", your self-esteem is improved and you treat yourself nicely trough "self-care." Modern Psychology also has ties with eastern religion through meditation. Psychology offers much life advice but none of it is from the Word of God. Its man attempts to be happy apart from what's taught in the Bible – a life with God as the provider of mental health.

You'll want to cut all ties to Psychology including books, programs and appointments.

To get free from Psychology, pray the following prayer.

In the name Jesus, by the blood of Jesus, I bring the cleansing blood of Jesus on me and my family for my involvement in Psychology [which includes... mention doctors and other psychological counseling including at hospitals] and [being a priest of Satan to influence others to seek Psychological treatment by word and by example].

In the name of Jesus and by the blood of Jesus, I renounce believing the lie that Psychology along with Psychiatry is my only hope for my suffering. The truth is God is now providing a detailed deliverance from Him. I praise the Lord for His blessing. In the name of Jesus, I command that lie to go to the Abyss and never return.

In the name of Jesus and by the blood of Jesus, I renounce believing the lie that all I need in life is to "cope" better. Jesus came so that I might be free by His blood. In the name of Jesus, I command that lie to go to the Abyss and never return.

In the name of Jesus and by the blood of Jesus, I renounce believing the lie that all I need in life is to have a high self-esteem. My self-esteem comes from being a child of God. In the name of Jesus, I command that lie to go to the Abyss and never return.

In the name of Jesus and by the blood of Jesus, I renounce believing the lie that I need to set boundaries for myself and not serve people the way Jesus did. Jesus washed the disciples' feet and died on the cross for our sins. In the name of Jesus, I command that lie to go to the Abyss and never return.

In the name of Jesus and by the blood of Jesus, I renounce believing the lie that I just need to treat myself well through self-care including hobbies, pastimes, and other comforts. Jesus said to deny yourself. In the name of Jesus, I command that lie to go to the Abyss and never return.

In the name of Jesus and by the blood of Jesus, I renounce believing the lie that if I can talk to my inner child, which is a lie and a demon. There should not be any conscience being in myself except myself. Any conversations with my "inner child" are conversations with demons. In the name of Jesus, I command that lie to go to the Abyss and never return.

In the name of Jesus and by the blood of Jesus, I renounce believing the lie that I need to defeat negative self-talk. There should not be any conscience being in myself except myself. Any conversation going on in my mind other than myself is either God or demons. The self-talk will go away when I'm done with the deliverance. In the name of Jesus, I command that lie to go to the Abyss and never return.

In the name of Jesus, by the blood of Jesus, I break the covenant I made with Satan, by being a priest of Satan in that way and my general involvement in that sin.

In the name of Jesus, by the blood of Jesus, I break the generational curse of Psychology off me and my family.

In the name of Jesus, by the blood of Jesus, I break the curse of Psychology off me and my family.

In the name of Jesus and by the blood of Jesus, I command a spirit of [counselor name] to go directly to the Abyss and never return. (Repeat for all doctors)

In the name of Jesus and by the blood of Jesus, I command a spirit of Psychology to go directly to the Abyss and never return.

In the name of Jesus and by the blood of Jesus, I command a spirit of [list counselors] to go directly to the Abyss and never return. (Do this for each counselor separately.)

Psychiatry

Psychiatry is another area to receive deliverance from. God has mercy on people when they're on medication, but God's better plan is deliverance even the deliverance found in this book.

Psychiatry comes with problems because it advocates psychological counselling. Also, every medication has actual curses as side-effects. There are a large number of possible side-effects or curses for the medication. There are curses because God wants people to pursue Him through deliverance to be free. Also, every Psychiatrist or assistant has a demon that comes through him.

The effects of these demons can actually make the person worse off than before and receive more mental illness. Generally, people aren't getting completely free. They're still under God's curse that will only be completely lifted until they step away from Psychology and Psychiatry and receive deliverance.

Here's a prayer for freedom.

In the name of Jesus, by the blood of Jesus, I bring the cleansing blood of Jesus on me and my family for my involvement in in Psychiatry including all of the visits, hospitalizations, PHP's and IOP's. I confess that I believed the lie that it was my only hope. I praise the Lord that He is now leading me through being delivered from mental health demons. [I also bring the blood on me being a priest of Satan in word and example for Psychiatry by influencing others to be involved in Psychiatry].

In the name of Jesus and by the blood of Jesus, I renounce believing the lie that Psychiatry along with Psychology is my only hope for my suffering. The truth is God is now providing a detailed deliverance from Him. I praise the Lord for His blessing. In the name of Jesus, I command that lie to go to the Abyss and never return.

In the name of Jesus and by the blood of Jesus, I renounce believing the lie that medicine can cure mental illness. I declare that only God can give me true freedom in Christ. In the name of Jesus, I command that lie to go to the Abyss and never return.

In the name of Jesus, by the blood of Jesus, I break the covenant I made with Satan [when I was a priest of Satan in that way] and my general involvement in that sin.

In the name of Jesus, by the blood of Jesus, I break the generational curse of Psychiatry off me and my family.

In the name of Jesus, by the blood of Jesus, I break the curse of Psychiatry off me and my family.

In the name of Jesus, by the blood of Jesus, I command a spirit of Psychiatry to go directly to the Abyss and never return.

In the name of Jesus, by the blood of Jesus, I command a spirit of [list medications] to go directly to the Abyss and never return. (Do this for each medication separately.)

In the name of Jesus, by the blood of Jesus, I command a spirit of [list doctors and assistants] to go directly to the Abyss and never return. (Do this for each doctor or assistant separately.)

Overall Prayers

At this point, it would be wise to seek some initial freedom from mental health demons and try casting them out. That could give you some relief of your symptoms until you have completed the deliverance and can repeat the process in full.

In the name of Jesus and by the blood of Jesus, I command a spirit of psychosis to go directly to the Abyss and never return.

In the name of Jesus and by the blood of Jesus, I command a spirit of schizophrenia to go directly to the Abyss and never return.

In the name of Jesus and by the blood of Jesus, I command a spirit of bi-polar to go directly to the Abyss and never return.

In the name of Jesus and by the blood of Jesus, I command a spirit of mania to go directly to the Abyss and never return.

In the name of Jesus and by the blood of Jesus, I command a spirit of borderline personality to go directly to the Abyss and never return.

In the name of Jesus and by the blood of Jesus, I command a spirit of anxiety to go directly to the Abyss and never return.

In the name of Jesus and by the blood of Jesus, I command a spirit of depression to go directly to the Abyss and never return.

In the name of Jesus and by the blood of Jesus, I command a spirit of OCD to go directly to the Abyss and never return.

In the name of Jesus and by the blood of Jesus, I command a spirit of suicide to go directly to the Abyss and never return.

In the name of Jesus and by the blood of Jesus, I command a spirit of homicide to go directly to the Abyss and never return.

OCD Deliverance

There's an OCD demon that is a consequence of sin. The demon has helper demons that help enslave the person with lies or obsessive thoughts. The lies or obsessive thoughts take the form of demons themselves and are extremely hard to overcome without casting out.

To get a full deliverance, it's best to complete the deliverance and then pray against a spirit of OCD and the lies. In the meantime, we casted out a spirit of OCD in the previous section. That stands. As you notice a lie, cast it out. Say something to the effect of:

In the name of Jesus, by the blood of Jesus, I confess and renounce the lie [name lie]. [Declare the truth]. In the name of Jesus, by the blood of Jesus, I command that lie to go directly to the Abyss and never return.

Sin Area: The Occult

The world has been deceived by the occult. Magic and sorcery are condemned in scripture. Revelation talks about people practicing "magic arts" going to Hell.

*[6] He said to me: "It is done. I am the Alpha and the Omega, the Beginning and the End. To the thirsty I will give water without cost from the spring of the water of life. [7] Those who are victorious will inherit all this, and I will be their God and they will be my children. [8] But the cowardly, the unbelieving, the vile, the murderers, the sexually immoral, those who practice **magic arts**, the idolaters and all liars—they will be consigned to the fiery lake of burning sulfur. This is the second death."* [3]

Halloween

Halloween is an evil holiday. Children like it because they can dress up and eat candy. However, many of the costumes are of evil creatures and they exalt death, darkness and the occult.

Halloween should be repented of and deliverance performed. When you bring the blood of Jesus onto the sin, be sure to confess these things:

- ❒ The costumes you dressed up in even as a child.
- ❒ Giving out candy.
- ❒ Eating the candy

---

[3] *The New International Version*. (2011). (Re 21:6–8). Grand Rapids, MI: Zondervan. (Emphasis added)

- ☐ Carving pumpkins
- ☐ Any haunted houses
- ☐ Horror shows and movies about Halloween or watched on the day
- ☐ Any home or yard decorations
- ☐ Any debauchery on this day including drinking and sexual sin
- ☐ Any other related sin that the Holy Spirit brings to mind

If you orchestrated any of these things for you and your family, be sure to confess being a priest of Satan.

An alternate holiday to celebrate is Nov 1 All Saints Day. Dress up as your favorite Bible character. Prepare a special meal. Invite friends and family to your celebration. Read scripture, pray and sing Christian songs.

Here's a sample prayer:

In the name of Jesus and by the blood of Jesus, I bring the cleansing blood of Jesus on me and my family for my involvement in Halloween. First, I bring under the blood me being a priest of Satan in [say any leadership]. I also bring under the blood, my involvement which included [list all involvement.]

In the name of Jesus and by the blood of Jesus, I renounce believing the lie that Halloween is an innocent holiday. In the name of Jesus, I command that lie to go to the Abyss and never return.

In the name of Jesus and by the blood of Jesus, I break the covenant I made with Satan by being a priest of Satan in this way and my general involvement in this sin.

In the name of Jesus and by the blood of Jesus, I break the generational curse of Halloween off me and my family.

In the name of Jesus and by the blood of Jesus, I break the curse of Halloween off me and my family.

In the name of Jesus and by the blood of Jesus, I command a spirit of Halloween to go directly to the Abyss and never return.

Christmas

Christmas is supposed to be about Jesus. Magic is part of some Christmas characters. Many depictions of Santa Clause include the use of magic. The reindeer supposedly fly because of magic. Frosty the snowman is shown as being powered by a magic hat.

However, the historical account of St. Nicholas bears repeating. He gave gifts of gold to women at their window so that their father could have a dowery for their marriages. Incorporating a tradition that lines up with the historical account instead of the magic is advised. You could have stockings and stocking stuffers and tell the account of the historical Saint Nicholas with your family. Use your best discernment as you create a Christian culture for you family.

The play/movie Christmas Carol presents ghosts instead of angels. The story presents a false gospel in that you can be saved through works.

The movie the Grinch Who Stole Christmas also presents a false gospel that you can be saved by honoring Christmas. The Christmas store at Disney contains no ornaments that point to Christ. Be sure to bring the blood on any participation in any Christmas magic elements.

- ❒ Gifts from Santa
- ❒ Decorations that include these occultic movies, cartoons or characters.
- ❒ Movies and cartoons watched
- ❒ Visits to the Disney Christmas store

Also be sure to confess being a priest of Satan if you organized any of this with your family. Before you try to break any of these curses, be sure to rid your household of any items pointing to a false gospel or magic with characters such as Santa Clause.

Because of Frosty the Snowman, there are many depictions of alive snow men. You should rid any of these from your home. You should bring the blood of Jesus on these as well and break the curse magic snowmen.

It should be noted that the practice of White Elephant parties should be avoided since they mock the present that God gave us in Jesus. It also mocks the gifts of the magi to Jesus at the manger.

When you are free, take time to pray and think about how you can make Christmas about Christ and not presents and occultic Christmas elements. I believe that the Holy Spirit will guide you and bless your future Christmas celebrations.

You can pray the following prayer:

In the name of Jesus and by the blood of Jesus, I bring the cleansing blood of Jesus on me and my family for my involvement in the following occultic practices at Christmas including [name practice]. I also bring under the blood being a priest of Satan in [name the way].

In the name of Jesus and by the blood of Jesus, I renounce believing the lie that I can celebrate Christmas without Christ. In the name of Jesus, I command that lie to go to the Abyss and never return. (Repeat for more than one lie.)

In the name of Jesus and by the blood of Jesus, I break the covenant I made with Satan [by being priest of Satan in that way] and my general involvement in the sin.

In the name of Jesus and by the blood of Jesus, I break the generational curse of Santa, the occult and magic off me and my family.

In the name of Jesus and by the blood of Jesus, I break the curse of the Santa, the occult and magic off of me and my family.

In the name of Jesus, by the blood of Jesus, I command a spirit of Santa to go directly the Abyss and never return.

In the name of Jesus, by the blood of Jesus, I command a spirit of magic to go directly the Abyss and never return.

The Easter Bunny

The resurrection of Jesus Christ has taken a back burner in America to the Easter Bunny. You should bring the blood on you and your family for practicing the Easter Bunny which could include the following:

- ❏ Telling children the myth of the Easter Bunny
- ❏ Chocolate Easter Bunnies

You can pray the following prayer:

In the name of Jesus and by the blood of Jesus, I bring the cleansing blood of Jesus on me and my family for my involvement in the following occultic practices including [name practices]. I also bring the blood on me being a priest of Satan in [name the ways].

In the name of Jesus and by the blood of Jesus, I renounce believing the lie that I can celebrate Easter without Jesus Christ. In the name of Jesus, I command that lie to go to the Abyss and never return. (Repeat for more than one lie.)

I the name of Jesus and by the blood of Jesus, I break the covenant I made with Satan by being priest of Satan in that way and my general involvement in the sin.

In the name of Jesus and by the blood of Jesus, I break the generational curse of the Easter Bunny, occult and magic off me and my family.

In the name of Jesus and by the blood of Jesus, I break the curse of the Easter Bunny, the occult and magic off of me and my family.

In the name of Jesus, by the blood of Jesus, I command a spirit of the Easter Bunny to go directly the Abyss and never return.

In the name of Jesus, by the blood of Jesus, I command a spirit of magic to go directly the Abyss and never return.

Occultic Practices

It's important to note that some of the actual practices, like magic, can be done through going through the act even if it's pretended. For example, someone may perform a magic trick that's pretend. That's still involvement in magic. Or, in playing games, if you or your player or character, practiced magic or occultic practice you're still guilty of that sin. Therefore, read through each of the occult practices and make sure you weren't involved in some way.

Be sure to confess at least the following that you were involved in:

- ☐ Magic
- ☐ Spells
- ☐ Levitation
- ☐ Telekinesis
- ☐ Hexes
- ☐ Omens
- ☐ Seances
- ☐ Ouija boards
- ☐ Occult websites
- ☐ Movies with the occult including ghosts
- ☐ Books of the occult
- ☐ Book stores

You can pray the following prayer:

In the name of Jesus and by the blood of Jesus, I bring the cleansing blood of Jesus on me and my family for my involvement in the following occultic practices including [name practice]. I also bring under the blood me being a priest of Satan in [name the ways].

In the name of Jesus and by the blood of Jesus, I renounce believing the lie that I can have power that doesn't come from God. In the name of Jesus, I command that lie to go to the Abyss and never return. (Repeat for more than one lie.)

I the name of Jesus and by the blood of Jesus, I break the covenant I made with Satan by being priest of Satan in that way and my general involvement in the sin.

In the name of Jesus and by the blood of Jesus, I break the generational curse of occult, magic and witchcraft off me and my family.

In the name of Jesus and by the blood of Jesus, I break the curse of the occult, magic and witchcraft off of me and my family.

In the name of Jesus, by the blood of Jesus, I command a spirit of [each specific sin e.g., telekinesis one at a time] to go directly the Abyss and never return. (Pray this section for each sin)

In the name of Jesus, by the blood of Jesus, I command a spirit of magic to go directly the Abyss and never return.

In the name of Jesus, by the blood of Jesus, I command a spirit of witchcraft to go directly the Abyss and never return.

Disney

Disney is involved in the occult and sorcery. Many of the movies including Frozen depict characters that practice magic. Their theme park is called the Magic Kingdom.

Before prayer, you should rid you and your family of all items related to Disney including toys, movies, Christmas ornaments, etc.

You should bring the blood of Jesus on all of your involvement with Disney. This could include the following:

- ❑ Being a priest of Satan and organizing watching Disney media or trips to the theme parks
- ❑ Movies watched
- ❑ Watching the Disney channel
- ❑ Songs sung

- ❏ Theme parks visited
- ❏ Cartoons
- ❏ Visiting the fake Disney Christmas store

You can pray the following prayer:

In the name of Jesus and by the blood of Jesus, I bring the cleansing blood of Jesus on me and my family for my involvement in the following Disney activities [name activities]. I also bring under the blood being a priest of Satan in [name the ways].

In the name of Jesus and by the blood of Jesus, I renounce believing the lie that I can find happiness apart from God. In the name of Jesus, I command that lie to go to the Abyss and never return. (Repeat for more than one lie.)

I the name of Jesus and by the blood of Jesus, I break the covenant I made with Satan by being priest of Satan in that way and my general involvement in the sin.

In the name of Jesus, by the blood of Jesus, I break the generational curse of sorcery, magic, witchcraft and the occult off me and my family.

In the name of Jesus and by the blood of Jesus, I break the curse of sorcery, magic, witchcraft and the occult off of me and my family.

In the name of Jesus, by the blood of Jesus, I command a spirit of magic to go directly the Abyss and never return.

In the name of Jesus, by the blood of Jesus, I command a spirit of sorcery to go directly the Abyss and never return.

In the name of Jesus, by the blood of Jesus, I command a spirit of witchcraft to go directly the Abyss and never return.

Dungeons and Dragons

Dungeons and Dragons is a very evil game. It includes characters that use magic. Also, role playing characters can be evil, have false gods and have spiritual power from false gods.

To gain freedom through Jesus for Dungeons and Dragons, pray this following prayer:

In the name of Jesus by the blood of Jesus, I bring the cleansing blood of Jesus on me and my family for my involvement in Dungeons and Dragons. [I bring under the blood me being a priest of Satan, through leadership in the game and being a dungeon master for the following occasions [list occasions]]. I also bring under the blood my involvement with being a character(s) in the game specifically [list characters]. [I confess and renounce that my player was neutral or evil.] I confess and renounce that my character(s) were druids, monks, paladins, or clerics with a false god and had spiritual power. I confess and renounce having a false God for other characters. I confess and renounce that my character practiced magic spells including [list spells]. I confess and renounce that my characters had false gods outlined in the Deity and Demigods manual. [In the name of Jesus by the blood of Jesus, I also bring under the blood of Jesus my involvement of playing characters that were thieves or assassins]. I bring all this involvement in Dungeons and Dragons under the cleansing blood of Jesus.

In the name of Jesus by the blood of Jesus, I bring the blood of Jesus on me and my family for my involvement in the Players manual, the Monster manual, the Deity and Demigods manual and the Dungeon Master manual. I bring the images of each page including the covers under the cleansing blood of Jesus. I also bring under the blood, the demon monsters that inhabit different levels of hell including such monsters that had nudity.

I bring under the blood all involvement in monsters, gods, and demigods that had nudity.

I also bring under the blood, the murder of characters and monsters including the pursuit of treasure. I confess and bring under the blood of Jesus, the different races including elves, hobbits and dwarves.

I bring under the blood the following monsters [list monsters that you remember.] I confess and bring under the blood my involvement with all dragons and creatures of hell.

I bring under the blood all the time and money I spent on the game including so called modules and figurines.

In the name of Jesus and by the blood of Jesus, I renounce believing the lie that I can play at false god worship, magic, and witchcraft and not come under judgement. In the name of Jesus, I command that lie to go to the Abyss and never return. (Repeat for more than one lie.)

In the name of Jesus by the blood of Jesus, I break the covenants I made with Satan by being a priest of Satan in that way and my general involvement in that sin.

In the name of Jesus, by the blood of Jesus, and by the authority given to me by Jesus and the full approval of the Trinity, I break the generational curse of Dungeons and Dragons, sorcery, magic, witchcraft and false religion off me and my family.

In the name of Jesus, by the blood of Jesus, I break the generational curse of Dungeons and Dragons, sorcery, magic, witchcraft and false religion off me and my family.

In the name of Jesus by the blood of Jesus, and by the authority given to me by Jesus and the full approval of the Trinity, I break the curse of Dungeons and Dragons, sorcery, magic, witchcraft and false religion off me and my family.

In the name of Jesus, by the blood of Jesus, under the authority given to me by Jesus and under the full approval of the Trinity, I break the curse of the occult, false religion, witchcraft, sorcery, infirmity, blindness, deafness and insanity off me and my family.

In the name of Jesus, by the blood of Jesus, I command a spirit of Dungeons and Dragons to go directly to the abyss and never return.

In the name of Jesus, by the blood of Jesus, I command a spirit of sorcery to go directly to the abyss and never return.

In the name of Jesus, by the blood of Jesus, I command a spirit of magic to go directly to the abyss and never return.

In the name of Jesus, by the blood of Jesus, I command a spirit of witchcraft to go directly to the abyss and never return.

In the name of Jesus, by the blood of Jesus, I command a spirit of false religion to go directly to the abyss and never return.

Fantasy Movies, TV Shows, Games and Books

Fantasy games and books can have some of the same problems as Dungeons and Dragons. Characters can use magic, sorcery and witchcraft or exert spiritual power from false gods. All of this needs to come under the blood.

Before doing the deliverance prayer, rid you household of all fantasy games and fantasy books.

In the name of Jesus, by the blood of Jesus, I bring the cleansing blood of Jesus on my involvement in fantasy movies, TV shows, games, and books that included occultic and/or false worship elements which included [list specific movies, shows, games and books, characters, and evil plots].

In the name of Jesus and by the blood of Jesus, I renounce believing the lie that I can play at or read about magic, sorcery, and witchcraft and false worship and not come under judgement. In the name of Jesus, I command that lie to go to the Abyss and never return. (Repeat for more than one lie.)

In the name of Jesus, by the blood of Jesus, I break the covenant I made with Satan with being a priest of Satan in that way and my general involvement in that sin.

In the name of Jesus, by the blood of Jesus, I break the generational curse of fantasy games, magic, sorcery, witchcraft, and false worship off me and my family.

In the name of Jesus, by the blood of Jesus, I break the curse of fantasy games, fantasy books, magic, sorcery, witchcraft, and false worship off me and my family.

In the name of Jesus, by the blood of Jesus, I command a spirit of fantasy games to go directly to the Abyss and never return.

In the name of Jesus, by the blood of Jesus, I command a spirit of fantasy books to go directly to the Abyss and never return.

In the name of Jesus, by the blood of Jesus, I command a spirit of magic to go directly to the Abyss and never return.

In the name of Jesus, by the blood of Jesus, I command a spirit of sorcery to go directly to the Abyss and never return.

In the name of Jesus, by the blood of Jesus, I command a spirit of witchcraft to go directly to the Abyss and never return.

In the name of Jesus, by the blood of Jesus, I command a spirit of false worship to go directly to the Abyss and never return.

J.R.R. Tolkien's The Hobbit and Lord of the Rings

Lord of the Rings and the Hobbit are evil in a variety of ways. They present the use of magic including magic practiced by the so called "good" characters. Any involvement including the books and movies requires a cleansing by the blood of Jesus as well as the breaking of a covenant, and curses.

In the name of Jesus by the blood of Jesus, I bring the cleansing blood of Jesus on me and my family for my involvement in the Lord of the Rings in books and movies including me being a priest of Satan and encouraging others to be involved. I also bring under the blood the magic and sorcery of the story. I also bring under the blood the use of "ghosts" for battle. I also confess and renounce the character Gandolf and the daughter of Elrond. I confess and renounce the magic ring and magic swords.

In the name of Jesus and by the blood of Jesus, I renounce believing the lie that Christian themes can be portrayed using elements of the occult. In the name of Jesus, I command that lie to go to the Abyss and never return. (Repeat for more than one lie.)

In the name of Jesus and by the blood of Jesus, in the authority given to me by Jesus and the full approval of the Trinity, I break the covenant I made with Satan for me being a priest of Satan in that way and my general involvement in the sin.

In the name of Jesus and by the blood of Jesus, I break the generational curse of witchcraft, magic, the occult, sorcery, and ghosts off me and my family.

In the name of Jesus and by the blood of Jesus, in the authority given to me by Jesus and the full approval of the Trinity, I break the curse of witchcraft, magic, the occult, sorcery, and ghosts off me and my family.

In the name of Jesus and by the blood of Jesus I command a spirit of the Lord of the Rings to go directly to the abyss and never return.

In the name of Jesus and by the blood of Jesus I command a spirit of the magic to go directly to the abyss and never return.

In the name of Jesus and by the blood of Jesus I command a spirit of the sorcery to go directly to the abyss and never return.

In the name of Jesus and by the blood of Jesus I command a spirit of ghosts to go directly to the abyss and never return.

CS Lewis' The Lion, the Witch and the Wardrobe Series

While there is some good in this series, there are some evil aspects to this book series and movies. The wood wardrobe that takes the children to Narnia, is from the planting of a magic tree. In addition, one of the children casts a spell using a wizard's spell book. Also, there is the depiction of witches practicing magic and sorcery. And the wizard is depicted as being a servant of Asland who is supposed to represent Christ.

In the name of Jesus and by the blood of Jesus. I bring the cleansing blood of Jesus on my involvement in the Lion, the Witch and the Wardrobe series in books and movies. I bring the blood also on me being a priest of Satan and leading people to be involved themselves. I confess and renounce the wardrobe, the spell, the depicted witches and the wizard.

In the name of Jesus and by the blood of Jesus, I renounce believing the lie that Christian themes can be taught using occultic means. In the name of Jesus, I command that lie to go to the Abyss and never return. (Repeat for more than one lie.)

In the name of Jesus and by the blood of Jesus, I break the covenant I made with Satan by [being a priest of Satan in this way] and my general involvement in that sin.

In the name of Jesus and by the blood of Jesus, I break the generational curse of magic, sorcery, witchcraft, the occult and The Lion, the Witch and the Wardrobe off me and my family.

In the name of Jesus and by the blood of Jesus, I break the curse of magic, sorcery, witchcraft, the occult and The Lion, the Witch and the Wardrobe off me and my family.

In the name of Jesus and by the blood of Jesus, I command a spirit of the Lion, Witch and the Wardrobe to go directly to the abyss and never return.

In the name of Jesus and by the blood of Jesus, I command a spirit of the magic to go directly to the abyss and never return.

In the name of Jesus and by the blood of Jesus, I command a spirit of the sorcery to go directly to the abyss and never return.

In the name of Jesus and by the blood of Jesus, I command a spirit of the witchcraft to go directly to the abyss and never return.

Harry Potter

Harry Potter is an evil book and movie series. It portrays young people practicing sorcery. It encourages young people to be involved in the magic and sorcery. If you have been involved in any way, you need to cleanse yourself by the blood of Jesus and break the covenant, lies and curses.

Before doing the deliverance prayer, rid you household of everything related to Harry Potter including books and movies.

In the name of Jesus and by the blood of Jesus, I bring the cleansing blood of Jesus on me and my family for my involvement in Harry Potter. [I confess being a priest of Satan where I encouraged people to either read the book, go to the Harry Potter attraction in Orlando, or watch the movies.] I also bring under the blood my general involvement in that sin including [reading the books], [going to the movies], [going to the theme park attraction] [toys and all objects related to Harry Potter]. [I also bring under the blood casting spells to copy what characters in the book did.]

In the name of Jesus and by the blood of Jesus, I renounce believing the lie that I can watch people practicing magic and sorcery and not come under God's judgement. In the name of Jesus, I command that lie to go to the Abyss and never return. (Repeat for more than one lie.)

In the name of Jesus and by the blood of Jesus, I break the covenant I made with Satan by being a priest of Satan in that way. I also confess my general involvement in that sin.

In the name of Jesus, by the blood of Jesus, I break the generational curse of witchcraft, sorcery, magic, and Harry Potter off me and my family.

In the name of Jesus and by the blood of Jesus, I break the curse of witchcraft, sorcery, magic, and Harry Potter off me and my family.

In the name of Jesus and by the blood of Jesus, I command a spirit of Harry Potter to go directly to the abyss and never return.

In the name of Jesus and by the blood of Jesus, I command a spirit of witchcraft to go directly to the abyss and never return.

In the name of Jesus and by the blood of Jesus, I command a spirit of sorcery to go directly to the abyss and never return.

In the name of Jesus and by the blood of Jesus, I command a spirit of magic to go directly to the abyss and never return.

Overall Occult Prayer

Now that you have been cleansed of your involvement in the occult, cast out a spirit of the occult.

In the name of Jesus, by the blood of Jesus I bring all forgotten and unmentioned involvement in the Occult under the blood of Jesus.

In the name of Jesus, by the blood of Jesus, I break the curse of the occult off me, my family, my house or apartment, off every object in my dwelling, and off my career.

In the name of Jesus and by the blood of Jesus, I command a spirit of the occult to go to the Abyss and never return.

In the name of Jesus and by the blood of Jesus, I command a spirit of Satanism to go to the Abyss and never return.

Sin Area: Secret Societies

Involvement in secret societies must be repented of. Such societies include fraternities and sororities, Freemasonry, The Moose, etc. These societies have non-Christian, even evil oaths, rites, and rituals. Freemasonry actually has ties to Satanism. All involvement in these organizations can bring demons. The details of involvement in these societies need to be confessed and brought under the blood of Christ. It is important to note that you should pray these prayers even if you only have ancestors who were in the secret society. You'll need to confess the sin and break the generational curse.

Freemasonry

In the name of Jesus and by the blood of Jesus, I bring the cleansing blood of Jesus on me and my family for my involvement in Freemasonry. I bring the blood of Jesus on the oaths, rituals, rites, and symbols including [remembered oaths, rituals, rites, and symbols] that I agreed to and participated in. I confess and renounce the Eastern mysticism and its ties to Satanism.

I bring the blood of Jesus on all of this involvement including all the time going to meetings and all the dark secrecy.

I also bring under the blood the leadership roles I had in Freemasonry when I led others and acted as a priest of Satan in that way.

In the name of Jesus and by the blood of Jesus, I renounce believing the lie that I can have righteousness without God. In the name of Jesus, I command that lie to go to the Abyss and never return. (Repeat for more than one lie.)

In the name of Jesus and by the blood of Jesus, I break the covenant I made with Satan by being a priest of Satan in that way and my general involvement in Freemasonry.

In the name of Jesus and by the blood of Jesus, I break the generational curse of Freemasonry and Satanism off me and my family.

In the name of Jesus and by the blood of Jesus, I break the curse of Freemasonry and Satanism of me and my family.

In the name of Jesus and by the blood of Jesus, I command a spirit of Freemasonry to go directly to the Abyss and never return.

In the name of Jesus and by the blood of Jesus, I command a spirit of Satanism to go directly to the Abyss and never return.

Moose Lodge and Others

In the name of Jesus and by the blood of Jesus, I bring the cleansing blood of Jesus on me and my family for my involvement in [lodge name]. I bring the blood of Jesus on the oaths, rituals, rites and symbols, including [remembered oaths, rituals, rites, and symbols] that I agreed to and participated in. I confess and renounce the Eastern mysticism and its ties to Satanism.

I bring the blood of Jesus on all of this involvement including all the time going to meetings and all the dark secrecy.

I also bring under the blood the leadership roles I had in [lodge name] when I led others and acted as a priest of Satan in that way.

In the name of Jesus and by the blood of Jesus, I renounce believing the lie that I can have knowledge and righteousness apart from God. In the name of Jesus, I command that lie to go to the Abyss and never return. (Repeat for more than one lie.)

In the name of Jesus and by the blood of Jesus, I break the covenant I made with Satan by being a priest of Satan in that way and my general involvement in [lodge name].

In the name of Jesus and by the blood of Jesus, I break the generational curse of [lodge name] and Satanism off me and my family.

In the name of Jesus and by the blood of Jesus, break the curse of [lodge name] and Satanism off me and my family.

In the name of Jesus and by the blood of Jesus, I command a spirit of [lodge name] to go directly to the Abyss and never return.

In the name of Jesus and by the blood of Jesus, I command a spirit of Satanism to go directly to the Abyss and never return.

Fraternity Prayer

In the name of Jesus, by the blood of Jesus, I bring the cleansing blood of Jesus on me and my family for my involvement in a fraternity specifically the fraternity of [name]. I bring the blood of Jesus on the oaths, rituals, rites, and symbols, including [remembered oaths, rituals, rites, and symbols]. I confess and renounce the secret handshakes, the hazing, the rings and other jewelry, the tattoos, and the secret ceremonies including the dark robes worn by the brothers. I also renounce and bring under the blood of Jesus, the debauchery, drunkenness, fornication, pornography, drug use and general ungodliness and sin practiced by the members of the group and specifically [list personal sins] that I participated in.

I also bring under the blood the leadership roles I had in [fraternity name] when I led others and acted as a priest of Satan in that way.

In the name of Jesus and by the blood of Jesus, I renounce believing the lie that I can have friendships with unbelievers and that I won't be corrupted by evil associations. In the name of Jesus, I command that lie to go to the Abyss and never return. (Repeat for more than one lie.)

In the name of Jesus, by the blood of Jesus, I break the covenant that I made with Satan [when I was a priest of Satan in that way] and my general involvement in the sin.

In the name of Jesus, by the blood of Jesus, I break the generational curse of fraternity involvement and the occult off me and my family.

In the name of Jesus, by the blood of Jesus, I break the curse of fraternity involvement and the occult off me and my family.

In the name of Jesus, by the blood of Jesus, I command a spirt of [fraternity name] to go directly to the Abyss and never return.

Sin Area: New Age and Eastern Religion

Star Wars

Star Wars is a New Age film. It's based on a New Age book. It presents a false view of dualism — that good and evil are diametrically opposed. It presents a false gospel in that if we operate under the so-called "Force," we can be good and be saved. However, this presents a false view of God. The all-powerful force in the universe is God and the Spirit of God goes out from the Father. And Jesus and the Father are one. And, only those who believe in the Lord Jesus Christ, will be saved.

There is no equivalent for evil. Evil is a perversion of good. There is no "dark side" of an equal and opposite force of evil. Evil is limited to man's sin and the influence of demons who gain control through sin.

To confess Star Wars, we must bring it under the blood in a prayer like the following:

In the name of Jesus, by the blood of Jesus, I bring the cleansing blood of Jesus on [me being a priest of Satan and leading my family in the watching of the movie] by me watching the movie(s). I confess and renounce Yoda, Luke Skywalker, Hans Solo, Princess Leia, Darth Vader and the evil emperor. I bring the blood on that scene and [that scene for as many scenes as you can remember.] I confess and renounce the Force and the phrase "May the Force be with You." I renounce the telekinesis, the light saber, the council of Jedi's and so-called dark side of the force. I confess and renounce the music that has a worshipful quality. I confess and renounce all Star Wars books, toys, and movies.

In the name of Jesus and by the blood of Jesus, I renounce believing the lie that evil is the opposite of good, and equally powerful. In the name of Jesus, I command that lie to go to the Abyss and never return.

In the name of Jesus and by the blood of Jesus, I renounce believing the lie that I can channel an impersonal force and do good. In the name of Jesus, I command that lie to go to the Abyss and never return. (Repeat for more lies.)

In the name of Jesus, by the blood of Jesus, I break the covenant I made with Satan by being a priest of Satan in that way and my general involvement in those movies and books.

In the name of Jesus and by the blood of Jesus, I break the generational curse of Star Wars off me and my family.

In the name of Jesus and by the blood of Jesus, I break the curse of Star Wars off me and my family.

In the name of Jesus and by the blood of Jesus, I command a spirit of Star Wars to go directly to the Abyss and never return.

In the name of Jesus and by the blood of Jesus, I command a spirit of the force to go directly to the Abyss and never return.

In the name of Jesus and by the blood of Jesus, I command a spirit of new age to go directly to the Abyss and never return.

In the name of Jesus and by the blood of Jesus, I command a spirit of incest to go directly to the Abyss and never return.

In the name of Jesus and by the blood of Jesus, I command a spirit of lust to go directly to the Abyss and never return

Yoga

Yoga has become prevalent these days. But Yoga is tied to Eastern Religion. All of the poses of Yoga are worship positions of false Gods. That makes Yoga a practice of false religion and false worship. Use the following prayer to gain freedom from Yoga. Before praying the prayer be sure to rid your property of all forms of Yoga which includes Yoga mats and blocks. Also, any videos with Yoga should also be removed from the property.

In the strong name of Jesus, I confess and renounce Yoga and all its practices. I confess and renounce its ties to eastern religion, philosophies and beliefs. I confess and renounce all religious phrases used in the videos. I confess and renounce the positions including the so-called death pose. The poses are tied to eastern, false religion and I want no part in them. I renounce the deep breathing as a practice of eastern religion. I am a blood bought Christian and I have the mind of Christ and want no part in eastern, false religion. I renounce all yoga videos and trips to yoga facilities. I renounce the stretching, the yoga mat and the yoga block.

In the name of Jesus by the blood of Jesus, I bring the cleansing blood of Jesus on me and my family for [my involvement as a priest of Satan leading others to yoga] and my involvement in yoga including all positions and poses, breathing, the videos, stretching, and the so-called death pose and being an active participant in yoga.

In the name of Jesus and by the blood of Jesus, I renounce believing the lie that I can use eastern religion to stretch and become flexible. In the name of Jesus, I command that lie to go to the Abyss and never return. (Repeat for more than one lie.)

In the name of Jesus by the blood of Jesus, I break the covenant I made with Satan when I was a priest of Satan in this way and my general involvement in that sin.

In the name of Jesus, by the blood of Jesus, I break the generational curse of Yoga off me and my family.

In the name of Jesus by the blood of Jesus, I break the curse of yoga off me and my family.

In the name of Jesus by the blood of Jesus, I command a spirit of death to go directly to the Abyss.

In the name of Jesus by the blood of Jesus, I command a spirit of false religion to go directly to the Abyss and never return.

In the name of Jesus by the blood of Jesus, I command a spirit of the Eastern religion to go directly to the Abyss and never return.

In the name of Jesus by the blood of Jesus, I command a spirit of yoga to go directly to the Abyss and never return.

Meditation

Meditation involves repeating a mantra over and over again while sometimes listening to relaxing music. Guided meditation involves visualizing something in particular for the purpose of obtaining peace. The goal of transcendental meditation is to empty oneself of self and becoming nothing or becoming part of the so-called universe. This practice is clearly evil and should be avoided. Any involvement requires bringing it under the Blood of Jesus.

In the name of Jesus and by the blood of Jesus, I bring the cleansing blood of Jesus on me and my family for [and me being a priest of Satan and inviting others to meditate or advocating meditation] and my general involvement with meditation during the following occasions [list occasions].

In the name of Jesus and by the blood of Jesus, I renounce believing the lie that I can become nothing or one with the universe. In the name of Jesus, I command that lie to go to the Abyss and never return. (Repeat for more than one lie.)

In the name of Jesus and by the blood of Jesus, I break the covenant I made with Satan [by being a priest of Satan in that way] and my general involvement in that sin.

In the name of Jesus by the blood of Jesus, in the authority given to me by Jesus I break the generational curse of meditation off me and my family.

In the name of Jesus and by the blood of Jesus, in the authority given to me by Jesus I break the curse of meditation off me and my family.

In the name of Jesus and by the blood of Jesus, I command a spirit of meditation to go directly to the Abyss and never return.

New Age Medicine

New Age Medicine includes alternative supplements that are tied to Chinese and Indian religion. They advance the lie that food that we eat is not nutrient rich enough to support us thereby creating a need for supplements.

Natural medicine stores can be a place where eastern religion and new age books, magazines and newspapers are distributed. Such stores should be confessed, renounced, and avoided.

In the name of Jesus and by the blood of Jesus, I bring the cleansing blood of Jesus on me and my family for my involvement with [list supplements] and being a priest of Satan in advocating the use of supplements to friends and family and church. I also bring under the blood my trips to health food stores and web sites related to new age medicine.

In the name of Jesus and by the blood of Jesus, I renounce believing the lie that food should be supplemented. In the name of Jesus, I command that lie to go to the Abyss and never return. (Repeat for more lies.)

In the name of Jesus and by the blood of Jesus, I break the covenant I made with Satan by being a priest of Satan in this way and my general involvement in New Age Medicine.

In the name of Jesus and by the blood of Jesus, I break the generational curse of New Age Medicine off me and my family.

In the name of Jesus and by the blood of Jesus, I break the curse of New Age Medicine off me and my family.

In the name of Jesus and by the blood of Jesus, I command a spirit of New Age Medicine to go directly the Abyss and never return.

New Age Churches, Crystals and Spirit Guides

There are churches for the New Age. Crystals are commonly used and spirit guides are given legal right to torment the subject.

In the name of Jesus and by the blood of Jesus, I bring the cleansing blood of Jesus on me and my family for being a priest of Satan and inviting friends and family to New Age churches and attending such churches myself. I also bring under the blood my involvement with crystals and so-called spirit guides. I also bring under the blood the following involvement including [list ways you've been involved in the New Age.]

In the name of Jesus and by the blood of Jesus, I renounce believing the lie that life can be found apart from the Lord Jesus Christ. In the name of Jesus, I command that lie to go to the Abyss and never return. (Repeat for more than one lie.)

In the name of Jesus and by the blood of Jesus, I break the covenant with Satan for being a priest of Satan in this way and my general involvement in that sin.

In the name of Jesus and by the blood of Jesus I break the generational curse of attending New Age churches, crystals and so-called spirit guides.

In the name of Jesus and by the blood of Jesus I break the curse of attending New Age churches, crystals and so-called spirit guides.

In the name of Jesus and by the blood of Jesus, I command a spirit of my so-called spirit guide to go directly to the Abyss never return.

In the name of Jesus and by the blood of Jesus, I command a spirit of the New Age to go directly to the Abyss and never return.

Overall New Age Prayer

Now that you've been cleansed of your involvement pray this general prayer.

In the name of Jesus, by the blood of Jesus I bring all forgotten and unmentioned involvement in the New Age and eastern religion under the blood of Jesus.

In the name of Jesus, by the blood of Jesus, I break the curse of the New Age and eastern religion off me, my family, my house or apartment, off every object in my dwelling, and off my career.

In the name of Jesus and by the blood of Jesus, I command a spirit of the New Age to go to the Abyss and never return.

In the name of Jesus and by the blood of Jesus, I command a spirit of Eastern Religion to go to the Abyss and never return.

In the name of Jesus and by the blood of Jesus, I command a spirit of Satanism to go to the Abyss and never return.

Sin Area: False Worship

³ "You shall have no other gods before me.
⁴ "You shall not make for yourself a carved image, or any likeness of anything that is in heaven above, or that is in the earth beneath, or that is in the water under the earth. ⁵ You shall not bow down to them or serve them, for I the Lord your God am a jealous God, visiting the iniquity of the fathers on the children to the third and the fourth generation of those who hate me, ⁶ but showing steadfast love to thousands of those who love me and keep my commandments. ¹ Ex 20:3–6, ESV

People were made for worship. That worship can be either true worship – worshiping the triune God of the Bible – or false worship worshiping something else.

Superheroes

Superheroes are a form of false worship. They are little gods that society idealizes for the superpower, strength and body form. Marvel Comics has character Thor who is considered to be a "god" along with his father Oden. Spiderman is based on an occult symbol of spiders. The Spiderman character has a false gospel of "With great power comes great responsibility." This implies that the viewers somehow have great power and is a poor substitute for the true gospel of Jesus Christ.

Batman is based on another occultic symbol of bats. The movies show him with actual bats. Batman is also disturbingly dark. And the villains are extremely evil.

There's also immorality in the movies and TV shows. Ironman is a womanizer and is depicted as have sex with a woman and lusts after a stripper. In the Marvel Comics TV show, Agents of Shield, characters have sex with each other out of wedlock. The TV show Flash depicts a couple living together. And Supergirl depicts Supergirl's sister in having a lesbian affair. The TV show Arrow also depicts characters having sexual affairs with each other.

In the name of Jesus and by the blood of Jesus, I bring the cleansing blood of Jesus on me and my family for [me being a priest of Satan in my involvement in getting others to watch superhero movies and TV shows. I also bring my general involvement in this sin under the blood of Jesus. I confess and renounce the false gospel of the movies and TV shows as well as the darkness and evil portrayed. I also bring under the blood the immorality depicted in this media.

In the name of Jesus and by the blood of Jesus, I break the covenant I made with Satan by being a priest of Satan in this way and by my general involvement in this sin.

In the name of Jesus and by the blood of Jesus, I break the generational curse of superheroes off me and my family.

In the name of Jesus and by the blood of Jesus, I break the curse of superheroes off me and my family.

In the name of Jesus and by the blood of Jesus, I command a spirit of Superhero worship to go directly to the Abyss and never return.

In the name of Jesus and by the blood of Jesus, I command a spirit of False Worship and worship to go directly to the Abyss and never return.

In the name of Jesus and by the blood of Jesus, I command a spirit of the occult to go directly to the Abyss and never return.

People Worship

In many ways, people can become the idols. That can include everything from spouse or girlfriend/boyfriend worship to parent worship, pastor worship, sports worship, and movie or music star worship. It can also include self-worship and trying to get others to worship us.

In the name of Jesus by the blood of Jesus, I bring the cleansing blood of Jesus on me and my family for the different ways I acted as a priest of Satan in leading others into people worship including myself. I also bring the blood on me and my family for worshiping [my spouse, girlfriend, boyfriend, parents, pastors, sports athletes, and movie and music stars.]

In the name of Jesus and by the blood of Jesus, I break the covenant I made with Satan by being a priest of Satan in this way and my general involvement in the sin of people worship.

In the name of Jesus and by the blood of Jesus, I break the generational curse of people worship off me and my family.

In the name of Jesus and by the blood of Jesus, I break the curse of people worship off me and my family.

In the name of Jesus and by the blood of Jesus, I command a spirit of people worship to go directly to the Abyss and never return.

Business Worship

Business worship can take many forms. It can include the love of money, position, and title. It can also manifest in starting a business and worshiping the business. Other forms of business worship include periodicals glamorizing business. There is nothing wrong with having a business as long as it's run on Godly principles including Proverbs and not an object of worship itself or simply a means to get rich.

In the name of Jesus and by the blood of Jesus, I bring the cleansing blood of Jesus on me and my family for my involvement in business worship. I confess and renounce [list involvement.] I also bring under the blood me being a priest of Satan by leading people to be involved in business worship.

In the name of Jesus and by the blood of Jesus, I break the covenant with Satan that I made when I was a priest of Satan in that way and my general involvement in business worship.

In the name of Jesus and by the blood of Jesus, I break the generational curse of business worship off me and my family.

In the name of Jesus and by the blood of Jesus, I break the curse of business worship off me and my family.

In the name of Jesus and by the blood of Jesus, I command a spirit of business worship to directly to the Abyss and never return.

Other Non-Christian Religions

There are a number of non-Christian Religions in the world. The following is a list of different types of false religion. Be sure to check off which ones you were involved in and use the list for prayer.

- ❐ Catholic
- ❐ Scientology
- ❐ Mormonism
- ❐ Israeli pagan worship including Baal, Molech worship and Asherah poles
- ❐ Muslim
- ❐ Hindu
- ❐ Buddhist
- ❐ India false gods
- ❐ Yoga — including mats and blocks
- ❐ Greek mythology
- ❐ Roman mythology
- ❐ Egyptian religion

- ☐ Mayan religion
- ☐ Native American religion
- ☐ Eskimo false worship
- ☐ African false worship
- ☐ Great Britain native people false worship
- ☐ Druids
- ☐ Irish false worship
- ☐ South America false worship
- ☐ Central America false worship
- ☐ Canadian native people false worship
- ☐ Australian aborigines
- ☐ Other pagan religions
- ☐ Stonehenge
- ☐ Pagan shrines — Hindu, Buddhist, India gods
- ☐ Buddhist monks
- ☐ Ancestor worship

In the name of Jesus and by the blood of Jesus, I bring the cleansing blood of Jesus on me and my family for me being priest of Satan and encouraging others to engage in false worship and my general involvement in false worship [including <list false religions>].

In the name of Jesus and by the blood of Jesus, I break the covenant I made with Satan for being a priest of Satan in that way and my general involvement in false worship.

In the name of Jesus by the blood of Jesus, I break the generational curse of false religion off me and my family.

In the name of Jesus by the blood of Jesus, I break the curse of false religion off me and my family.

In the name of Jesus by the blood of Jesus, I command a spirit of [list specific false religion] to go directly to the Abyss and never return. (Repeat for each one)

Food Worship/Gluttony

People can worship different types of food. For some it may be coffee or desserts. For others it may be too much fine dining. Food was meant to taste good, but over emphasizing it can be food worship. Certain companies can emphasize their food as something to worship.

Gluttony can take the shape of eating too much food. You should eat until you are full, no more.

In the name of Jesus and by the blood of Jesus, I bring the cleansing blood of Jesus on me and my family for my involvement in food worship including [instances including coffee, dessert, too much fine dining, and <list others>] and me being a priest of Satan and encouraging others to worship food.

In the name of Jesus and by the blood of Jesus, I break the covenant I made with Satan for me being a priest of Satan in that way and my general involvement with that sin.

In the name of Jesus and by the blood of Jesus, I break the generational curse of food worship and gluttony off me and my family.

In the name of Jesus and by the blood of Jesus, I break the curse of food worship and gluttony off me and my family.

In the name of Jesus and by the blood of Jesus, I command a spirit of food-worship to go directly to the Abyss and never return.

In the name of Jesus and by the blood of Jesus, I command a spirit of gluttony to go directly to Abyss and never return.

Overall False Worship Prayer

In the name of Jesus and by the blood of Jesus, I break the generational curse of False Worship off me and my family.

In the name of Jesus and by the blood of Jesus, I break the curse of False Worship off me and my family.

In the name of Jesus and by the blood of Jesus, I command a spirit of False Worship to go directly to the Abyss and never return.

Sin Area: Sexual Sin

¹Follow God's example, therefore, as dearly loved children ² and walk in the way of love, just as Christ loved us and gave himself up for us as a fragrant offering and sacrifice to God.

*³ **But among you there must not be even a hint of sexual immorality, or of any kind of impurity**, or of greed, because these are improper for God's holy people. ⁴ Nor should there be obscenity, foolish talk or coarse joking, which are out of place, but rather thanksgiving.⁴ Eph 5:1–4, NIV (Emphasis added)*

Lust is an evil spirit that must be dealt with. It's important that you confess all of your sin in this area to get free. Other demons come from a spirit of lust to form unGodly soul ties that have to be broken also.

There are several forms of sexual sin including the following:

- ☐ Pornography
- ☐ Lust
- ☐ Fornication — sex outside marriage
- ☐ Masturbation
- ☐ Anal sex
- ☐ Gay or lesbian sex
- ☐ Lustful sex with your spouse
- ☐ Making out with other people besides your spouse.

In the name of Jesus and by the blood of Jesus, I bring the cleansing blood of Jesus on me and my family for ungodly sex including:

---

⁴ *The New International Version.* (2011). (Eph 5:1–4). Grand Rapids, MI: Zondervan.

Viewing pornography during on these occasions including [list occasions.]

Lusting after these people [list people.]

Fornication on these occasions including [list occasions.]

Masturbation on these occasions including [list occasions.]

Anal sex on these occasions including [list occasions.]

Gay and lesbian sex on these occasions including [list occasions.]

Making out with people who weren't my spouse on these occasions including [list occasions.]

All lustful sex with my spouse on these occasions including [list occasions.]

I also bring under the blood the times where I led others to participate in sexual sin on these occasions including [list occasions.]

In the name of Jesus and by the blood of Jesus, I break the covenant with Satan that I made by being a priest of Satan in this way and my general involvement in the sin.

In the name of Jesus, by the blood of Jesus, I confess and renounce the lie that I can find happiness apart from God. In the name of Jesus, by the blood of Jesus, I command that lie to go directly to the Abyss and never return. (Repeat for more than one lie.)

In the name of Jesus and by the blood of Jesus, I break the generational curse of sexual immorality, adultery, lust, perversion, and pornography off me and my family.

In the name of Jesus and by the blood of Jesus, I break the curse of sexual immorality, adultery, lust, perversion, and pornography off me and my family.

In the name of Jesus and by the blood of Jesus, I command a spirit of lust to go directly to the Abyss and never return.

In the name of Jesus and by the blood of Jesus, I command a spirit of pornography to go directly to the Abyss and never return.

In the name of Jesus and by the blood of Jesus, I command a spirit of masturbation to go directly to the Abyss and never return.

In the name of Jesus and by the blood of Jesus, I command a spirit of gay and lesbian sex to go directly to the Abyss and never return.

In the name of Jesus and by the blood of Jesus, I command a spirit of anal sex to go directly to the Abyss and never return.

In the name of Jesus and by the blood of Jesus, I command a spirit of perversion to go directly to the Abyss and never return.

Ungodly Soul Ties/Adultery

Ungodly soul ties can be formed by too much intimacy between unmarried persons. Inappropriate sharing may take the form too much talk about the family, sharing hopes and dreams, travel with members of the opposite sex that includes lengthy conversations, or too much time spent talking in a one-on-one meeting. With too much contact an ungodly soul tie can form even in the form of coveting your neighbor's wife or adultery of the heart. Ungodly soul ties can also form through reading books or listening to worship music by a member of the opposite sex. At its worse, such contact can lead to affairs or infidelity. Ungodly soul ties can be easily entered when there's a spirit of lust in your life.

It's important to bring the blood of Jesus on such sin and break the soul tie.

In the name of Jesus and by the blood of Jesus I bring the cleansing blood of Jesus on me and my family for forming an ungodly soul tie with [person(s)]. In the name of Jesus, I break the soul tie.

In the name of Jesus and by the blood of Jesus, I break the generational curse of adultery off me and my family.

In the name of Jesus and by the blood of Jesus, I break the curse of adultery off me and my family.

In the name of Jesus and by the blood of Jesus, I command a spirit of adultery to go directly to the Abyss and never return.

Overall Sexual Sin Prayer

In the name of Jesus and by the blood of Jesus, I break the generational curse of Sexual Sin off me and my family.

In the name of Jesus and by the blood of Jesus, I break the curse of Sexual Sin off me and my family.

In the name of Jesus and by the blood of Jesus, I command a spirit of Sexual Sin to go directly to the Abyss and never return.

Sin Area: Secular Media

Secular Music

All secular music should be avoided. Music was meant for worship. It was designed by God for the purpose of worshiping him.

Secular music leads people away from God by making them think that they can be saved, find significance or happiness through the songs they listen to. It's a false gospel. Many secular songs advocate immoral behavior or promote worshiping your spouse or boyfriend/girlfriend. Secular music also teaches ungodly and sinful values.

When you listen to secular music, you're listening to the music of Satan.

Many shops and restaurants play ungodly secular music. Such restaurants should be avoided in favor of wholesome home cooked meals.

Using the prayer in the prayer section, you should bring the various types of secular music under the blood of Jesus. You will need to call out specific bands, albums and songs.

In the name of Jesus by the blood of Jesus, I bring the cleansing blood of Jesus on me and my family for being a priest of Satan by playing secular music for my friends and family. I confess and renounce listening to Rock and Roll, Progressive, Rap, Jazz and Pop secular music. I also confess and renounce my own involvement in secular music. I bring the cleansing blood of Jesus on me and my family for watching videos with secular music.

I also bring the blood of Jesus on me and my family for all rock and roll music including [list bands, albums, singers, and songs.]

I also bring the blood of Jesus on me and my family for all progressive music including [list bands, albums, singers, and songs.]

I also bring the blood of Jesus on me and my family for all secular pop music including [list bands, albums, singers, and songs.]

I also bring the blood of Jesus on me and my family for all secular rap music including [list bands, albums, singers, and songs.]

I also bring the blood of Jesus on me and my family for all secular Jazz music including [list bands, albums, singers, and songs.]

In the name of Jesus, by the blood of Jesus, I confess and renounce the lie that I can find happiness apart from God. In the name of Jesus, by the blood of Jesus I command that lie to go directly to the Abyss and never return.

In the name of Jesus by the blood of Jesus, I break the covenant I made with Satan for being a priest of Satan in that way and my general involvement of listening to secular music.

In the name of Jesus by the blood of Jesus, I break the generational curse of secular music off me, my wife and my children.

In the name of Jesus by the blood of Jesus, I break the curse of secular music off me, my wife and my children.

In the name of Jesus by the blood of Jesus, I command a spirit of rock and roll music to go directly to the Abyss and never return.

In the name of Jesus by the blood of Jesus, I command a spirit of progressive music to go directly to the Abyss and never return.

In the name of Jesus by the blood of Jesus, I command a spirit of pop music to go directly to the Abyss and never return.

In the name of Jesus by the blood of Jesus, I command a spirit of jazz music to go directly to the Abyss and never return.

In the name of Jesus by the blood of Jesus, I command a spirit of rap music to go directly to the Abyss and never return.

In the name of Jesus, by the blood of Jesus, I command a spirit of secular music to go to the Abyss and never return.

Secular Movies and TV Shows

Secular movies and TV shows should be avoided as well. They advocate a false gospel of life without God. Also, it forms a yoking with people who aren't pursuing God. The Bible says not be yoked together with unbelievers. Secular movies and TV shows can produce such a yoking.

Secular movies and TV shows also teach ungodly values. Secular movies and TV shows can contain other elements such as language and nudity.

All involvement with secular movies and TV shows should be cleansed. In time, other movies and TV shows may come to mind. Such involvement should be cleansed as well.

In the name of Jesus and by the blood of Jesus, I bring the cleansing blood of Jesus on me and my family for being a priest of Satan and encouraging other people in watching secular movies and TV shows. I bring the following movies and TV shows under the blood including [list movies and TV shows.] I also confess watching movies and TV shows that were R or X rated and contained nudity including movies and shows that contain sexual immorality.

I also confess movies and TV shows that had strong language including taking the name of the Lord in vain. I confess and renounce the immorality of secular movies and TV shows in general including them practicing the occult, false religion superhero worship and sexual immorality. I also confess and renounce watching TV shows and movies with Martial Arts and eastern religion content.

In the name of Jesus and by the blood of Jesus, I break the covenant with Satan by being a priest of Satan in that way and my general involvement in that sin.

In the name of Jesus and by the blood of Jesus, I break the generational curse of secular movies and TV shows off me and my family.

In the name of Jesus and by the blood of Jesus, I command a spirit of secular movies to go directly to the Abyss and never return.

In the name of Jesus and by the blood of Jesus, I command a spirit of secular TV shows to go directly to the Abyss and never return.

In the name of Jesus and by the blood of Jesus, I command a spirit of lust to go directly to the Abyss and never return.

In the name of Jesus and by the blood of Jesus, I command a spirit of the occult to go directly to the Abyss and never return.

In the name of Jesus and by the blood of Jesus, I command a spirit of false religion and Satanism to go directly to the Abyss and never return.

Overall Secular Media Prayer

In the name of Jesus, by the blood of Jesus, I confess and renounce the lie that I can find happiness apart from God. In the name of Jesus, by the blood of Jesus, I command that lie to go directly to the Abyss and never return.

In the name of Jesus and by the blood of Jesus, I break the generational curse of Secular Media off me and my family.

In the name of Jesus and by the blood of Jesus, I break the curse of Secular Media off me and my family.

In the name of Jesus and by the blood of Jesus, I command a spirit of Secular Media to go directly to the Abyss and never return.

Sin Area: General Sin

The following sin are general sins that should be confessed.

- ☐ Greed
- ☐ Envy
- ☐ Gossip
- ☐ Slander
- ☐ Coveting your neighbor's wife or possessions
- ☐ Murder
- ☐ Hatred
- ☐ Violence
- ☐ Theft
- ☐ Unforgiveness/bitterness
- ☐ Obscenity
- ☐ Foolish talk
- ☐ Coarse joking
- ☐ Anger
- ☐ Malice
- ☐ Rage
- ☐ Yelling
- ☐ Discord
- ☐ Sloth/laziness
- ☐ Not providing for your immediate family

In the name of Jesus and by the blood of Jesus, I bring the cleansing blood of Jesus on me and my family for all instances of [sin] including [specific times.] I also bring under the blood those times when I encouraged or set an example of a sinful lifestyle acting as a priest of Satan in that way.

In the name of Jesus, by the blood of Jesus, I break the covenant by being a priest of Satan in that way and my general involvement with the sin.

In the name of Jesus and by the blood of Jesus, I break the generational curse of [list sins.]

In the name of Jesus and by the blood of Jesus, I break the curse of [list sins].

In the name of Jesus and by the blood of Jesus, I command a spirit of [sin area such as rage] (for all sin areas one at a time).

Curses

When sin is severe and it's warranted, the Lord extends a curse on that person's life. It's all part of His plan for the rebellious to turn to home. Many times, the curse can be related to the sin thought brought it. For example, let's say you've gossiped at work. The Lord may bring you a layoff. Or maybe you've committed adultery. The Lord may curse your marital intimacy and bring strife to your marriage relationship.

Now that you've worked through your sin confession and repentance, you can now look to the Lord to break the curses.

Curses can hide. When you have a curse, you can do something over and over again and have no idea that a curse is causing you to do that. Curses can also manifest as infirmities and sickness. Ask the Lord in prayer to reveal the curses you've been under. Once He does, you can then break the curse.

For each curse that is revealed to you, pray the following prayer:

In the name of Jesus, by the blood of Jesus, I break the generational curse of [infirmity or sin area]. (Break all of them one at a time.)

In the name of Jesus, by the blood of Jesus, I break the curse of [infirmity or sin area.] (Break all of them one at a time.)

In the name of Jesus, by the blood of Jesus, I command a spirit of [infirmity or sin area] to go directly to the Abyss and never return.

Curses could be strife in the marriage, problems on the job, different types of sickness or health conditions. Again, as you notice things through the Lord's prompting, break the curse under the blood of Jesus because Jesus became a curse for us by hanging on the cross. Now that we are cleansed, we have a basis to break the curse. If you haven't repented, the curse will remain in place.

Closing Prayer

In the name of Jesus, by the blood of Jesus, I command a spirit of deceit to go directly to the Abyss and never return.

Lord, I praise you and thank you for cleansing me. In the name of Jesus and by the blood of Jesus, I break the generational curse of Satanism off me and my family.

In the name of Jesus, by the blood of Jesus, I confess and renounce the lie that I can find happiness apart from God. In the name of Jesus, by the blood of Jesus I command that lie to go directly to the Abyss and never return.

In the name of Jesus and by the blood of Jesus, I break the curse of Satanism off me and my family.

In the name of Jesus and by the blood of Jesus, I command a spirit of Satanism to go directly to the Abyss and never return.

Lord, I pray that you would search me every day and let me know if anything doesn't please you.

I pray that you would have mercy on me and use me for building your kingdom.

Closing Prayer for Mental Health

In the name of Jesus and by the blood of Jesus, I break the generational curse of mental illness and insanity off me and my family.

In the name of Jesus and by the blood of Jesus, I break the curse of mental illness and insanity off me and my family.

In the name of Jesus and by the blood of Jesus, I command a spirit of psychosis to go directly to the Abyss and never return.

In the name of Jesus and by the blood of Jesus, I command a spirit of bi-polar to go directly to the Abyss and never return.

In the name of Jesus and by the blood of Jesus, I command a spirit of mania to go directly to the Abyss and never return.

In the name of Jesus and by the blood of Jesus, I command a spirit of borderline personality to go directly to the Abyss and never return.

In the name of Jesus and by the blood of Jesus, I command a spirit of anxiety to go directly to the Abyss and never return.

In the name of Jesus and by the blood of Jesus, I command a spirit of depression to go directly to the Abyss and never return.

In the name of Jesus and by the blood of Jesus, I command a spirit of OCD to go directly to the Abyss and never return.

In the name of Jesus and by the blood of Jesus, I command a spirit of suicide to go directly to the Abyss and never return.

In the name of Jesus and by the blood of Jesus, I command a spirit of homicide to go directly to the Abyss and never return.

Going Forward

Now that you have been cleansed, keep up your cleansing by keeping short accounts with the Lord. If you find yourself in sin, bring the blood of Jesus on it an apologize to anyone you hurt through the sin. You can use the general format of this book's prayers to bring sin under the blood, cast out lies, break covenants, break curses and cast out demons. You'll find that the Holy Spirit will use life experiences to remind you of sin for you to repent of. Pray that God would always show you ways that are displeasing to Him.

As you begin to serve God, you may get demons as assignments from the enemy. If you notice something unusual, pray that God would reveal what's going on. Then cast out the invading demon.

Now go and win souls for Christ. Lead them in righteousness and tell sinners to turn back to the Lord. Teach everyone what is in God's book the Bible. Strengthen your brothers with the Word.

Notes

Notes

Notes

Notes

Printed in the United States
by Baker & Taylor Publisher Services